REJOICING
in Him

PRAISES IN VERSE

REJOICING in Him

PRAISES IN VERSE

Roy Gardner

© 2003 by Roy Gardner. All rights reserved.

Printed in the United States of America

Packaged by Pleasant Word, a division of WinePress Publishing, PO Box 428, Enumclaw, WA 98022. The views expressed or implied in this work do not necessarily reflect those of Pleasant Word, a division of WinePress Publishing. Ultimate design, content, and editorial accuracy of this work are the responsibilities of the author.

No part of this publication may be reproduced, stored in a retrieval system, or transmitted in any way by any means—electronic, mechanical, photocopy, recording, or otherwise—without the prior permission of the copyright holder, except as provided by USA copyright law.

Unless otherwise noted, all Scriptures are taken from the Holy Bible, New International Version, Copyright © 1973, 1978, 1984 by the International Bible Society. Used by permission of Zondervan Publishing House. The "NIV" and "New International Version" trademarks are registered in the United States Patent and Trademark Office by International Bible Society.

Scripture references marked KJV are taken from the King James Version of the Bible.

Scripture references marked NASB are taken from the New American Standard Bible, © 1960, 1963, 1968, 1971, 1972, 1973, 1975, 1977 by The Lockman Foundation. Used by permission.

ISBN 1-57921-604-8
Library of Congress Catalog Card Number: 2003101385

Table of Contents

Acknowledgements 7
Foreword 9

My Savior 11
Thoughts 13
Submission 14
The Promise 17
Thoughts 19
A Giving God 20
A Sorrowful God 24
Thoughts 26
A Time to Serve 27
All Things New 30
Thoughts 32
Behold the Rose 33
Cheerfulness 37
Thoughts 38
Christ the Divine 39
A Day of Praise 43
Thoughts 44
A Sinless Earth 45
You Called Me 48

Thoughts	49
God's in Charge	50
His Light	54
Thoughts	55
His Presence	56
Not Forgotten	59
Thoughts	60
Praises	61
The Bridge	64
Thoughts	65
Faithful	66
Thoughts	68
His Grace	70
Thoughts	71
Of God	72
Our Kindness	75
Thoughts	76
The Great Event	77
The Carpenter	81
Thoughts	83
The King of Kings	84
The Lamb of God	87
Thoughts	88
Be Spirit Filled	89
Pure in Thought	92
Remaining Near	94
We Worship You	98
Thoughts	99
From God	100
Journey of Trust	105

Acknowledgements

Thanks be to God for giving me the inspiration for these writings and making it all come to fruition.

I wish to thank all my friends who gave me encouragement to continue this labor of love.

Many Thanks to Dave Harmon for the art work "Moments of Expressions" to Brian Parks for the author's portrait, and to Donald Dahn for "Journey of Trust"

Foreword

Jesus Christ is unquestionably the most important person to have ever lived. He has had more impact on human life than anyone who has ever walked this earth.

More has been written about Jesus than any other, because His mission on earth affected the lives of all people.

In His total innocence, Christ was subjected to humiliation; He was spurned, despised and rejected. When He gave His life at Calvary on the cross, His concern was for our soul's destiny. Jesus arose again, confirming His work which freed us from the bonds of sin.

The soul is the vital, spiritual nature of every person on earth; it is immortal, co-existent with the body and separable only at death. Those who trust in the atoning sacrifice of Jesus Christ will find forgiveness and eternal fellowship with God.

This writer has endeavored to express in verse the qualities of a loving and caring Savior. Christ's work on earth is a bridge between God and man; He became the propitiation for our sins.

Spiritual poems are a source of inspiration; a source that gives and keeps giving, because they are inspired by God, who is the center of all things.

In these tumultuous times, we desperately need a source of consolation and relief from our anxieties, grief, stress, and fear.

As a gift from God this writer hopes that others may also be inspired and that they may experience a deeper sense of security, and a feeling of peace and joy.

My Savior

When I tried to run my life, my days were fraught
with stress and strife,
Now that Christ leads my day, I feel a joy
along the way,
Joy fulfilling true and strong, that only God
can pass along.

By knowing Him through faith and trust, He takes
away the sin of lust,
And all the other sins and shame, He takes away
my blots and stains.

Though now not in the acts of sin, a sinner I
will always be,
If not for God's enduring power, my eyes though
open would not see.

I pray to follow in His path, although
His prints I cannot fill,
I want my actions every day to show His peace,
His love, His will.

He nurtures me and feeds my soul and leaves
this warmth within,

He gives me grace to keep me whole, where
once was only sin.

He loved me so beneath that sin while
hanging on that tree,
He died for me and rose again for all eternity.

Through the cross God pledged His love,
He gave His only Lamb,
He is Alpha and Omega; He is our God, "I Am."

Thoughts

At the closing of the day
My conscious heart set free;
My mind at rest, I've done my best
Much praise I give to Thee.

Submission

I stand in awe of God's presence as I rise
to meet the day,
Through the cross He bonded with us,
so we can walk in Eden's way.

Inherently vile and void within, on an
isle with merits none;
Helplessly lost without salvation, that
His death and victory won.

He bore the blame; He felt the sorrow, sin's
pain upon His brow,
Yet when they crucified our Savior,
He rose the victor now.

Let's put away the works of darkness and cloak
ourselves in His light,
And be the victor in the battle—not the
loser steeped in blight.

What awaits us on the morrow? Are our
lives in disarray?
We can be blessed and ready for Him if He comes
tomorrow, if He comes today.

For God so loved the world, that he gave his only begotten Son, that whosoever believeth in him should not perish, but have everlasting Life.

John 3:16

The Promise

We have the promise of life eternal, a
paradise in the sky,
A place of refuge in God's presence, we will
not sorrow, pain, or cry.

Oh for the light of life eternal, where the
sunshine never dies,
Word made flesh that dwells among us,
with steadfast heart we
can rely.

When we reach to talk with Jesus and
He seems yet far away,
Continued prayer is our answer, to get
back on His path today.

We reap the harvest of our sowing, sad as the
wind that sweeps the land,
Yet we can partake of His glory, feel the touch
of His gentle hand.

Let's cast our egos by the wayside and let
the humble ways abide,

And ever set our sights on Jesus, forever to
be by His side.

We like sheep have lost our bearings, lives torn
asunder bleak and void,
Yet we have complete assurance with total submis-
sion to our Lord.

Behold the glory of the heavens; see the
splendor of the sun,
Our heart's desire to see the Father, behold His
face when our race is won.

Thoughts

A kinder voice repeats itself
I hear it o'er and o'er.
It gently says "come unto Me."
"Fear not, I am standing at your door."

A Giving God

Can our hopes in God be gone, squandered
through the years?
To fade and fall and rot and die,
laden with our tears.

Can we see dewdrops on a rose, its
petals to be fed?
Or blossoms snowy on a tree, majestic
to be read?

Or winter nights in robes of white, bedecked
with silver stars?
Or radiant beauty of the dawn that
breaks night's prison bars?

O Lord, our God from up above, clothed
in Your brightest white,
We pray forgiveness through Your love,
majestic in Your light.

Knowing You is loving You, the One
who gives us life,
You grant us all these earthly joys, Your kingdom
and eternal life.

Blessed are the ears that hear the words
that You have said,
And blessed are the feet that walk the paths that
You have tread.

Verily I say unto you, except you be converted, and be-come as little children, ye shall not enter into the king-dom of heaven.

Matthew 18:3

A Sorrowful God

The seas behold His sorrow, the earth can
feel His plight,
He would that all men's souls be saved,
He arms us for the fight.

He dwells in realms of timeless being, the years
as moments passing by,
Seeing things beyond our seeing, unchanged
as eons dawn and die.

His sight today is the same tomorrow, as we
strive the victory will He keep,
Has He no tears for our sorrows, does
He not watch us as we sleep?

Does He not feed the hungry sparrow
and also give the rain?
He prays His Father to forgive us and
to free us of our shame.

Peace be to souls arriving into the
light where God appears,
Where the faithful will not waver, may
their eyes be dry of tears.

Come listen to His gentle pleading and
reap the joyful sound,
Let our new hearts do the leading, to know this
true love found.

Thoughts

The optimist finds opportunity in
everything he does,
The pessimist finds difficulty in everything
he tries to do.

A Time to Serve

Now is the time for labor and thought, a time
to serve not sin,
He gave us the light, He taught us His ways,
it's time we give praise to Him.

He gave us the beauty of this domain, He gave us
the darkness to sleep,
And all of the wonders of things on earth, He
wants us to smile not weep.

When He created this beautiful earth, a
paradise it was to be,
He gave us choices, we disobeyed Him; the
penalty now we see.

God saw the need to save our souls, so
to us He sent His Son,
The perfect and unblemished Lamb, with
His life the victory won.

So now it's time to awaken and to do
the things we can,
To remember what He did for us, remember
His nail-scarred hands.

Behold the Lamb of God, which taketh away the sin of the world.

John 1:29

All Things New

God made things new when He set us free, all
deeds written in His book,
We let Him lead with nail-pierced hands,
for all our sins He took.

We left the old path and are on the new, our
trials now with joy we know,
Christ gives to us the strength we need, the
faith to defeat the foe.

We seek our victories in Him, our
prayers will make it so,
When He gives us a task to do, how can
we tell Him no!

We were born to know God's love, life
has no other quest,
We rest assured in His love so pure,
without it we know no rest.

We pray to know more of His grace, and
seek a higher aim,

That we may better serve our Lord
and extol His holy name.

Unfettered by the sin and woe that earthly
things can bring,
In a constant search for grace, from great wells
our faith will spring.

Thoughts

If I have done an unkind deed,
Lord teach me to repent.
As You have taught in all Your words,
The message heaven sent.

Behold the Rose

I feast my eyes upon the rose, its beauty oh so
rare,
Its fragrance wafting through my mind, I
want to keep it there.

One unique and perfect thing, the sunshine
sought to mould,
Its beauty flaming like His love
with mystery I behold.

In God's creation of our earth there's
beauty to be read,
I see the tears of Christ inside, His blood
has dyed it red.

We like the beauty of the rose, tender petals
in our youth,
A perfect notion of His love meant
to thrive and grow in truth.

But like the short life of the rose,
its beauty blessed still,
Our lives will grow, our lives will fade,
as snow on summer's hill.

Yes like the rose our life will fade, to rest
in winter's strain,
Just as the season's fading months, to be
reborn again.

If we pursue His promised prize of
life's eternal fare,
Like the beauty of the rose we're
nurtured in His care.

Blessed are the poor in spirit: for their's is the kingdom
of heaven.

Matthew 5:3

Cheerfulness

If you have a spare smile today please
pass it on to me,
Don't keep it hid or under lid, I would
so happy be.

God gave us music in our hearts, He gave
us love to share,
He gave songs for us to sing that others
might know we care.

Don't keep kind words beneath your breath,
muffled in your heart,
This day will never come again, let now
your voice impart.

May the kindness of this hour be shared with
those you love,
And may we all show this kindness like
the spirit of a dove.

Extensions of God's love you know
have no limits, none for sure,
Spread your kindness, spread your love,
may it keep your spirit pure.

Thoughts

Oh what a mighty force is He
Creator of it all.
The first, the last, the greatest one
He makes the final call.

Christian the Divine

He who is Savior, Redeemer of life,
Gives us solace in times of strife,
Christ the maker and the giver,
Gives living water like a river.
His completeness.

Christ who loved and bore the cross,
Who suffered Himself to bear our loss,
A sinless life was glad to give,
That eternal life we could have to live.
His perfection.

He was so selfless in His love,
Came to bear our sin from above,
With tender feelings for our plight,
Himself exchanged for Adam's blight.
His feelings.

Those who knew His teachings He did trust,
Yet He saw them asleep at the dusk,
Then He prayed to God on high,
His desire to keep the Father nigh.
His patience.

As He trudged on with the cross,
Men's thoughts of Him were of loss,
Yet triumphantly He arose again,
And thwarted Satan's fated sin.
His fulfilling.

Behold, the fear of the Lord, that is wisdom; and to depart from evil is understanding.

Job 28:28

A Day of Praise

It's morn, we rise another day, the night
of rest is done,
A blessed day to praise His name, to see
His victories won.

A fresh new day, another chance
to show our faith in Him,
Another chance to greet someone,
to nod and smile to them.

One more day and best of all,
a time for us to use,
Time to praise and love our Lord, no time
to waste or lose.

We'd do well to use this day to fulfill
His good plan,
To use our hours, make them count,
for good of God and man.

Lord we ask You on this day and pray
You give us the light,
To go about Your business Lord
and carry on the fight.

Thoughts

Search my heart Lord
Keep me in good stead in things I say and do.
Keep me humble on my knees
With a spirit contrite and true.

A Sinless Earth

If I could and had the power,
I'd banish earth's sin and shame,
Give each soul peace and purpose,
Tell the world why Jesus came.

I'd take the world and bathe it,
And soothe it through the night,
I'd take away its cares and sorrows,
And make all wrong things right.

Yes I would cancel all its grieving,
Take away all wars and crime,
Trade all the bad for goodness,
Let it know just perfect times.

I'd take our errors like grain and thresh them,
Blow the chaff into the wind,
And make us pure and truly spotless,
Not to be remembered for our sin.

Wait! Jesus did this on Calvary,
He gave His life for me,
He died to cleanse the world of sorrow,
And rose again victoriously.

Blessed are the meek: for they shall inherit the earth.

Matthew 5:5

You Called Me

You called to me, You said my name,
O lover of my soul,
O Father who reigns on high,
You want my spirit whole.

When You speak I love to hear
Your call to mend my life,
At Your behest I do my best, You want me
free from strife.

I try to heed Your every plea, You give me
peace at night,
When I awake another day, I keep You
in my sight.

I pray forgiveness for my sins,
may I with love repent,
Receive Your understanding grace,
to me forgiveness sent.

Forever will I praise Your name and I'll extol
Your power,
Pray keep me in Your safety Lord
and make my tempter cower.

Thoughts

As I travel on my path
May everyone I meet
Know from my attitude
I see victory not defeat.

God's in Charge

If we lay aside the sinful way
Put His word to the test,
Our soul will rest in harmony
He will keep us at our best.

But if we bow to temptation's call
In everything we've sought,
The message of Satan's cause
Is the grief we've bought.

God is great and He is sure
He knows of all our needs,
When we stand before His throne
He will judge us by our deeds.

May we rebuke the tempter's lure
For all his works are naught,
We'll surely find no solace there
In the hell that he has wrought.

We know God's judgment swift and sure
And all His loving ways,

And if we keep our ramparts strong
He will help us through our days.

The music that we love to sing
Brings blessings to our ears,
And as we listen to His Word
It edifies our years.

Blessed are the peacemakers: for they shall be called the children of God.

Matthew 5:9

His Light

Engrossed in the world of sin and sorrow,
unaware of God's ways,
Never seeking, never looking to find
the meaning of His grace.

A shadowy ship, unreal and shapeless,
wallowing in an angry sea,
Mocking all my thoughts and senses,
working to envelop me.

Rearing as a dream in mocking, looming errors
in my thought,
Taking speed and gaining motion, 'till I think
that all is naught.

Then rises the light of His kindness, the anguish
of the night is gone,
He turns my dreary night to gladness,
turns my darkness into dawn.

In a twinkling His light can find me hid beneath
the blight of sin,
I need only heed His calling, to enter
in my heart and win.

Thoughts

Have I done my deed today,
Did I make one person smile?
Have I witnessed of my Lord,
Has my day been worthwhile?

His Presence

With Your presence oh so sweet, Oh the power
of Your love,
I see Your hand in every work
upon earth to far above.

The sun, the stars, the moon, all artworks
of Your being,
And all we know our eyes can't see
tells us of Your seeing.

I behold Your care shown in the rose, the dew
upon its leaf,
The tenderness of springtime youth, should we
not have belief?

Blessed be our Savior! Who I fear to be without,
Hosanna! Hosanna! Hosanna!
I hear the angels shout.

Blessed are the merciful: for they shall obtain mercy.

Matthew 5:7

Not Forgotten

God never promised painless lives,
all prosperous days or such,
Or things we think deserving, He gives His love,
His faith—so much.

Our way has trials and turmoil too and some days
mixed with strife,
Not only roses line our path, but with thorns
He tests our life.

He said we must endure some things
which we don't understand,
He said we need to trust in faith;
that He is in command.

In our trials and trouble too
let's pray for saving grace,
God has not forgotten us, He grooms us
in this place.

Thoughts

Did I give my praise to Thee
Extol Your holy name?
Or did I tread in worldly mire
And neglect my Savior came?

Praises

How many ways can I praise my Lord?
Many more than I know,
How many ways does He love me?
He's pure as the fallen snow.

I remember when He's been my guide,
when I could scarcely see,
And all the times He gave me peace, a friend
He'll always be.

What are the limits of His grace He's shown
since Adam's sin,
And does He not forgive me still
when I serve myself not Him?

The energy that comes from God
surrounds and fills the earth,
It surely has no limits, how can I judge its worth?

Eternal is my love for Him as He gives me
one more day,
And eternally I'll praise His name as He
prepares my way.

Verily, verily, I say unto you, he That believeth on me hath everlasting life.

John 6:47

The Bridge

His blood that flowed made peace with God
It cleansed the stains of sin.
Our souls have birth from the life He lived
When He bridged the gap for men.

With us in mind He filled the void
That gift only He could give.
To end the gulf 'twixt God and man
So we could eternally live.

The sin that taunts and mocks His love
And derides the peace He sought.
Is overruled and He prevails
Our peace with His life He bought.

His love bespeaks His noble work
His calm testifies of His will.
He answered when the need was great
He climbed up Calvary's hill.

Thoughts

Did I work for Christ today
Did I bring someone joy?
Was I His perfect tool
His honor to employ?

Faithful

As I reach to touch His garment, I remain
in yearning still,
I must be steeped in total faith and know
His total will.

Evil's power floods my day and through
the eve and night,
But it can't compare to the Spirit's power
or with the holy light.

My faith brings power to search His presence
and His face,
It guards my knowledge clean and pure,
to keep me in the race.

And when my race is finished and life here
is on the wane,
Pray keep me near Your bosom Lord, I praise
Your holy name

As Your blood flowed on the cross, You made
Your sacrifice,
The victory won with the unblemished Son,
You paid the total price.

Yes Lord, You made the promise; I know it
to be true,
Your will be done over evil You won, take me
home with You.

Thoughts

A Pearl

Things turn out best for those
who make the best of the way
things turn out.

His Grace

May God smile upon our path the way
that we should go,
And may He give us living joy
and let His blessings flow.

Let's give attention to our Lord
as He speaks His love,
Pray do not let our minds and thoughts
keep us from above.

Let's fix our course upon the Lord
while on this stormy sea,
Put all our trust in Him we must!
Sure will our compass be.

Lord take the "I" the "my" and "me"
and strike them to the ground,
fill us with "Thou" and "Thy" and "Thee"
and send us glory bound.

We cast our egos at your feet
and pray Your spirit start,
Our prayer within, free us from sin
that we be pure in heart.

Thoughts

We thank You Lord and praise Your name,
For in it we can find,
A lasting love,
A forever warmth,
And joy to sow in kind.

Of God

As we write of God we need not speak
"Things of Yore" or "Yesteryear"
He is not gone, He is here to stay.
Christ reigns!

He lives, He loves, He guides our life
He bid's us keep the faith
He gives us knowledge as we need.
His Bride!

It's not Christ "was" it's Christ "is,"
He is our shining ray of hope,
He is here to see, for all to know.
Omnipresent!

It's not that He can't fill our prayer,
And may take more time, we think!
He answers in the way He wants.
Omniscient!

The total sum of all He is
Is not a total after all
No limits does He know
The galaxies heed His call.
Omnipotent!

This is my beloved Son, in whom I am well pleased.

Matthew 3:17

Our Kindness

May our love flow, our kindness spread to one
and then the other,
Pray keep in memory to recall that person
is our brother.

It does not cost a single thing,
as free as the air we breathe,
As free as the love God gives to us,
a gift we all receive.

Why keep a joyous love inside,
hid and shielded there,
When we can give to all the world
what He has freely shared?

His giving knows no limits; His sharing
has no bounds,
God said in His word what we share
comes back around.

Thoughts

Christ gives me all this joy I feel
Have I kept it hid?
Have I shown His signs of love
In everything I did?

The Great Event

Does it seem too much and too good to be true
That He suffered the thorns, the cross,
and the pain?
The jeers and sneers and piercing spear
Satan's power Christ overcame.

Fervently praying in the garden
Amid sorrow and shame for our sin.
He awoke the sleeping disciples
Then to the Father He prayed again.

He suffered His way through evil's touch
Our savior a hero was He.
His precious blood flowed freely
As He was nailed to Calvary's tree.

The earth quaked, the veil was rent
Bespeaking His great worth.
The skies turned dark, the sun went black
Testifying of victory's birth.

The angel moved the stone away
Christ arose and sealed our trust.
His victory over sin that day
His power o'er Satan's thrust.

Christ arose, death lost its power
Salvation for us was won.
The Shepherd and the Lamb united
Christ's work on earth was done.

Faithfully Christ bore our burden
It could be borne by none but Him.
He finished this work on earth for us
So our cup could be filled to the brim.

Blessed are they that mourn for they shall be comforted.

Matthew 5:4

The Carpenter

A perfect man this Christ we love,
a carpenter by trade,
We look upon this universe His holy hands
have made.

As we behold the rainbow that arcs across the sky,
We know the hand that made this art
also made you and I.

Handprints of His are everywhere, in land,
and sky, and sea,
His boundless love from up above
touches you and me.

If we pause and question why His face
we cannot see,
One day through faith and trust we will, His
children all are we.

Infinitely He knew our needs on earth, the
wretched souls of all,
He freely gave His life that day to save us
from the fall.

Christ was such a humble man as He contended
for our lives,
He carried on His back that day the burden
of our strife.

When Christ wore that crown of thorns
what really came to bear,
Was not that crown of thorns He wore, but our
sins for which He cared.

He hung upon the cross that day, He bled
for you and me,
He paid the price, made the sacrifice, did this
to set us free.

Thoughts

When Christ was burdened with the cross,
Heavy laden with our sin,
Did we say we were sorry Lord,
Did we regret it then?

The King of Kings

Kings on earth were praised and worshiped,
and wore robes of velvet fine,
But the glory they knew has faded, they all
failed the test of time.

But lo the King of kings in heaven wore a
homespun robe that day,
The soldiers who gambled for this garment
will rue their fateful way.

He prayed Father take this cup if You will,
but He knew it could not be,
God knew the end from beginning
and Christ could also see.

When they laid Him in the tomb the stone
was placed to stay,
But with a tiny motion the angel
rolled that stone away.

He bore the pain, endured the sorrow,
and suffered their unbelief,
Let's praise His name! Exhort the King!
Who perished with the thief.

Blessed are the pure in heart: for they shall see God.

Matthew 5:8

The Lamb of God

When Jesus prayed in Gethsemane place, He was
pained through to the heart,
Still He went on in trust for He knew He must;
the end He knew from the start.

Our Christ who hung on the cross that day,
a blessing to me and you,
Pleased the Father through His work,
that none but He could do.

We love the rose with its beauty rare,
with mind and eyes that see,
But for us to truly love our Christ, our faith
must fully be.

Blessed are the souls that know the saga
of His strain,
And seek the path that pierced Him, that led
to victory's gain.

The beauty of this Lamb of God, He is
the perfect One,
He rules in robes of purest white and is wor-
shipped on His throne.

Thoughts

Lord I pray you prosper me,
In words and deeds and thought,
May I reflect Your meekness,
From the lessons You have taught.

Be Spirit Filled

Lord fill me with Your spirit, renew me every day,
That I may know You better, show me
the narrow way.

When I have erred in deed and thought and
brought You pain and tears,
Pray fill me with true faith dear Lord
as the Holy Spirit nears.

Your everlasting love for me, in every word
You said,
You came with light through darkness with
holy light You led.

With Your enduring spirit Lord, You seek me
with Your call,
I pray that You be near at hand
to redeem me when I fall.

I love You Lord and thank You and praise
Your holy name,
And when I come before You forgive me
of my shame.

And he saith to them, follow me, and I will make you fishers of men.

Matthew 4:19

Pure in Thought

When we are standing near the cross
we'll know our Savior best,
His loving light will shine on us,
His caring manifest.

With His glory ever about, the end
we do not know,
The glory of the universe, of heaven
and earth below.

His energy is bold and pure, it formed
space and earth,
It saturates our being, it was there before our birth.

His knowledge extending far and wide
our minds can never know,
Because we are finite and He is infinitely so.

Our Father knows our cares and woes,
He'll furnish as we need,
May we ever rest our faith in Him
and always let Him lead.

I turn my eyes to heaven and see His splendor fair,
It conjures up the warmest thoughts of all God's
angels there.

Remaining Near

Lord we come before You humbly seeking
forgiveness, love, and care,
And we know You hear and answer; if we pray
You are always there.

Pray fill us with Your Spirit, let our daily
trials be few,
Give us succor and living water so we
can be used by You.

Hold us to Your bosom Jesus, keep us wise
in all Your ways,
May we keep the Cross before us Lord, and be
true through all our days.

Lest we stray from Your teachings and fall away
from Your loving arms,
We pray You'll search and find us and keep us
free from harm.

Apportion to us O Lord we pray the peace
and joy we seek,
Pray that our eyes keep seeing and Your grace
will keep us meek.

But as it is written, eye hath not seen, nor ear heard, neither have entered into the heart of man, the things which God hath prepared for them that love him.

1 Corinthians 2:9

But God comendeth his love toward us, in that, while we were yet sinners, Christ died for us.

Romans 5:8

We Worship You

Now we come before You Lord
Seeking peace and grace.
As we love and honor You
Together in this place.

We arise to praise Your name
And exhort You in our song.
We pray You keep us in Your care
Free us from all things wrong.

You Lord are our safety net
In times of distress and need.
Our Rock of Salvation too
You bless our days indeed.

You show us how to love
And also how to pray.
You freely give more grace to us
More sunshine in our day.

Praise You Jesus! Praise Your name!
Teach us how to pray.
Help us know you better Lord
Show us now Your way.

Thoughts

If someone smote me on the cheek
Did I turn my head?
Or did I rebuff with anger
Because of what he did?

From God

The greatest gifts come from God,
this in His Word I read,
And I am nothing on my own but
filthy rags indeed.

True verse that falls upon my mind
from a source unseen,
Is given by His thoughts to me
and not by my mind seen.

He gives the thought, the verse, the flow,
in it His truth I find,
If not for God's great gifts of love, my mind
is truly blind.

The treasures that He has for me
I do not earn or know,
My solemn prayer is to write for God, in verse
His blessings flow.

I would that all may read and know and feel
the grace God shares,
And see the fullness of His love and know
how much He cares.

It tells us of His truth, His love, His peace,
and of His joy sublime,
I pray He shares more thoughts with me
and I'll pen them into rhyme.

Blessed are those which hunger and thirst after righteousness: for they shall be filled.

Matthew 5:6

Journey of Trust

Donald Dahn

Close your eyes and picture a beautiful, sunny day. You are steering a boat across a cobalt blue lake and turn back to see the billowing wake. The churning white water trailing behind the boat temporarily marks where you have traveled, until it disappears. The wake is not the force which propels the boat forward, nor is it the rudder that guides it, controlling the direction of travel. It is only the boiling, vanishing, watery trail of a past journey, temporarily recording the voyage of our choices.

We pilot our boat. We have the choice to steer our boat in a direction that can be good, not so good, or on a course which leads to destruction. If the wake shows us that we have been heading in the wrong direction, we are blessed with the freedom to turn the wheel at any time, and to head in the right direction. We can choose the course that God whispers in our ear—toward His promise of good for us. However, He has also given us the freedom to run full speed into a floating log and sink. And this could happen while we are looking back.

Clearly the wake has no power to propel the boat, nor does it posses any wisdom to guide the one who steers it. The wake only shows us the trail of our past navigational choices; maybe they were erroneous choices we made when we thought that we were the master of our destiny. But in God, this wake of our past has literally and figuratively vanished. It doesn't exist anymore, except as an image in our memory. Our past has no power over us, except the power we grant it. We are new creations in Christ; we can choose not to continue making the wrong choices that controlled our past thoughts and actions. Furthermore, we can put away the disturbing and depressing memories of our transgressions. In Him, we can deny them any power over us; only the evil one uses the condemnation of our failures to confuse us, and to undermine our faith.

Through the unfathomable love of Jesus, His Holy sacrifice, and His forgiving power, the transgressions of our past exist now only in our memory—not His; now we are in Him and they are no longer part of our life. We must pray for the strength to put away destructive memories; to deny them the power to affect the new course we have chosen. We must be still and listen, and gladly accept, submit to, and follow the guiding power of the Holy Spirit who lives within us. It is He we hear speaking to us now, guiding us on our new journey minute by minute, hour by hour of every day. We must pray to be constantly and vigilantly aware of God's love, mercy and grace; embracing these as our bright, redeeming, spiritual light—our new compass. This divine beacon will point with absolute certainty to a very precise and wonderful destination. Only He can give us the strength we require to follow our appointed course and to complete our journey in victory. This strength comes from Him; it does not exist in us.

An airplane flies off course more than ninety percent of the time during any journey. The path of the flight is not a straight line between two points; actually it is a series of very small course corrections which direct the aircraft safely to its destination. The diaphanous contrails drifting behind show only where the aircraft has traveled and while beautiful, are but a disappearing vapor in the jet stream. The pilot follows the flight plan, keeping his eyes locked on the ultimate goal, using his mind, disciplined perseverance, and the computerized navigational system. During our journey we make countless, small course corrections to successfully reach our predetermined destination. The pilot consciously chooses to place total faith, and the ultimate fate of the aircraft in the guidance system. He most certainly does not rely on his feelings—or the contrails to guide him. We must place our total faith in Jesus Christ, not in ourselves or the direction of our past.

We must not look back at the wake, the contrails, or the dust of our past journey. Now, in the present, we must trust God with all our hearts and minds; charging boldly forward into life, faithfully consulting with Him in prayer regarding all circumstances we face. He is the one true compass; only He has the power to guide our lives successfully. We must embrace Him with an open heart and an open mind, placing our trust in the navigational guidance of the Holy Spirit, who will faithfully lead us along the one true path. The path He has designated for each one of us; the path which will lead us to our promised destination in this world. When we finally arrive, and the work here is finished, the path will lead us home—into the loving arms of God The Father.

Man's ultimate and elusive quest for a successful, fulfilling life is attainable if we will open our hearts and minds to God, and accept His plan for each one of us. Above all we must love Him, live in His Word, and pray—not that our will—but His be done. Jesus, through the Holy Spirit, is the divine compass who will successfully and unerringly guide us on our journey. He also gives us the master key to unlock the power of His strength; His power—the power of almighty God, which promises us ultimate spiritual victory. We need His strength and His armor to engage, and to combat the forces of darkness which do their best to overtake us. We must have this strength to endure, and to be conquerors in these battles of spiritual warfare which we face daily. We are His children and His warriors. He loves us dearly; we need only ask for His help and He will gladly give it to us. God promises us victory, His victory, if we will only trust Him, loving each other along the way as he commands. He requires our love and trust before we can receive His power to endure our trials, His many gifts, and His protection. If we will surrender, and allow Him to direct our lives, our future is certain. God's plan for us is perfect, and wonderful beyond all imagining.

He will show us the way. He will give us His strength. Be still and listen, and know that He is God.

To order additional copies of

Have your credit card ready and call:

1-877-421-READ (7323)

or please visit our web site at
www.pleasantword.com

Also available at: www.amazon.com

Printed in the United States
61695LVS00002B/13-45

9 781579 216047